SQUANTO AND THE
FIRST THANKSGIVING

SQUANTO AND THE FIRST THANKSGIVING

BY JOYCE K. KESSEL

ILLUSTRATIONS BY LISA DONZE

On My Own

HOLIDAYS

Carolrhoda Books, Inc./Minneapolis

This book is available in two editions:
Library binding by Carolrhoda Books, Inc., a division of Lerner Publishing Group
Soft cover by First Avenue Editions, an imprint of Lerner Publishing Group
241 First Avenue North
Minneapolis, MN 55401 U.S.A.

Website address: www.lernerbooks.com

Library of Congress Cataloging-in-Publication Data

Kessel, Joyce K.
    Squanto and the first Thanksgiving / by Joyce K. Kessel ; illustrated by Lisa Donze. (Rev. ed.)
        p.   cm. — (On my own holidays)
    Summary: An introduction to the life of the Massachusetts Indian Squanto, best known for befriending the Pilgrims of the New Plymouth Colony.
    ISBN: 0–87614–941–7 (lib. bdg. : alk. paper)
    ISBN: 1–57505–585–6 (pbk. bdg. : alk. paper)
    1. Thanksgiving Day—Juvenile literature. 2. Squanto—Juvenile literature. 3. Wampanoag Indians—Biography—Juvenile literature. [1. Squanto. 2. Thanksgiving Day. 3. Pilgrims (New Plymouth Colony). 4. Wampanoag Indians—Biography. 5. Indians of North America—Massachusetts—Biography.] I. Donze, Lisa, ill. II. Title. III. Series.
GT4975 .K47 2004
394.2649—dc21   2002008316

Manufactured in the United States of America
2 3 4 5 6 – JR – 09 08 07 06 05 04

for Ric, Allison, and Sean
—J.K.K.

for my mother and father
—L.D.

For thousands of years, people have
set aside special days for giving thanks.
People in the United States have
celebrated Thanksgiving
for over 350 years.
How did Thanksgiving start?
Most people think it started
with the Pilgrims.
But the story really begins with a
Patuxet Indian named Squanto.
Without Squanto, the Pilgrims
would never have celebrated
that first Thanksgiving.

The Patuxet tribe lived
near the place
that became
Plymouth, Massachusetts.
There they grew corn and
hunted wild animals.
They were friendly and peaceful.

9

Then an English ship came to
Plymouth in the early 1600s.
These Englishmen were explorers.
They were looking for riches.
They hoped to find gold or silver.
But all they found was corn and Indians.
The Englishmen had never seen corn.
They didn't know what to do with it.
But they thought they knew what
to do with Indians.
They would sell them as slaves.

So the Englishmen captured a few
of the Patuxet men.
They put them on their ship.
They took them back to England.
Squanto was one of those men.

In England, Squanto had to learn
how to speak English.
He had to work very hard.
But Squanto was used to
hard work.

Winters in Plymouth had been
long and cold.
Sometimes, Squanto was
hungry all winter long.
But the rest of the year had
brought riches.
The woods of his home were full
of berries and wild animals.
And even when he was hungry,
he was free.

Squanto longed for his home.

He dreamed of his people and
of his wild, free land.

His master could see that Squanto
was not happy.

He felt sorry for his slave.

Finally, he set Squanto free.

In 1614, Captain John Smith sailed
for the New World.

Squanto went with him.

He returned at last to his people.

But not for long.

Captain Smith sailed back to England.

But he left one of his ships behind.

The captain of that ship was named

Thomas Hunt.

Hunt traded with the Patuxets.

He filled his ship with

fish and animal furs.

But Hunt was greedy.

He wanted to make more money

than the fish and furs would bring.

So he filled part of his ship with

Patuxet men.

Squanto was captured again.

After only a few weeks at home,

he was sailing back across the ocean.

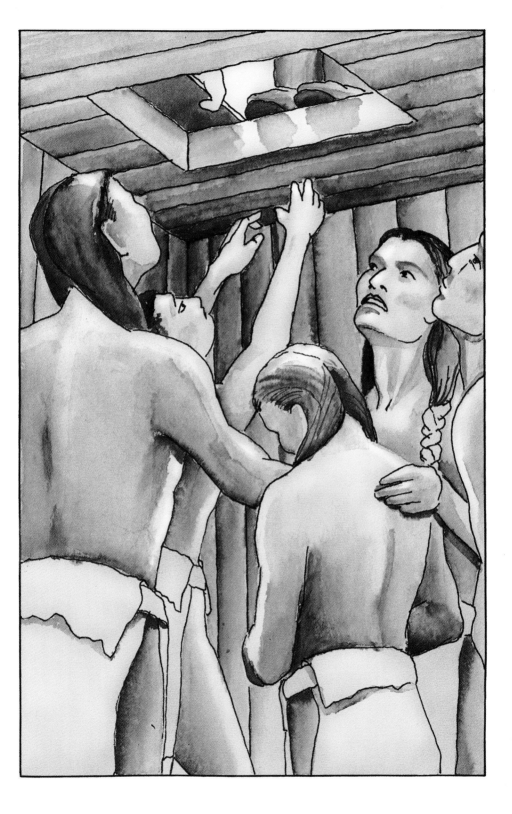

Hunt knew that Captain Smith
would be angry with him for
capturing the Patuxets.
So Hunt sold the Patuxets in Spain
instead of England.

Squanto's new masters were
Catholic monks.
They taught him the Christian faith.
They were kind to him.
But Squanto was sadder than ever.
All he wanted was his freedom.
At last the monks took pity on him.
They helped him get to England.

In England, Squanto was able to
find a ship going to America.
He was on his way home again!
But what great sadness he found
when he arrived.
Squanto wandered through
Patuxet villages.
He could not believe his eyes.
All he found were empty huts.
The cornfields were black and dead.
All of his people were gone.
Squanto was the only living Patuxet.

What had happened?

A nearby tribe told him.

The ships from England had
brought smallpox germs.

Smallpox was a new disease to
the Patuxets.

They died quickly from it.

The disease had killed all of them.

After all those years of longing for his
home, Squanto found he had no home.

He moved in with the nearby tribe.

The Pilgrims landed at Plymouth
on December 21, 1620.
Squanto had been back for one year.
The Pilgrims were English.
They had left England to look
for a new home.
They wanted to live where they could
worship the way they chose.
They were lucky to land at Plymouth.
The Indians there were afraid of smallpox.
They would not fight for their land.
The Indians just watched from a distance.

The Pilgrims had a hard time.
They did not know how to plant.

They did not know how to build.
They made cold little houses out
of mud, clay, and sticks.

They were not used to the cold.

They did not have much to eat.

Half of the Pilgrims died during
their first terrible winter.

By the spring of 1621, there were
only 55 of them left.

That was when Squanto decided
to help the Pilgrims.
He knew how to speak English.
He could tell them what to do.
In 1621, Squanto went
to visit the Pilgrims.
After his first visit, he never left them.

Squanto taught the Pilgrims how to
find animals to shoot for meat.
He showed them how to build
warm houses.
He helped them make friends with
nearby Indians.
Squanto showed the Pilgrims
how to plant.
He told them to watch the leaves
on the trees.
When they were as big as a
squirrel's ear, the corn should be planted.
He taught the Pilgrim women how
to cook the corn.

Squanto and the Pilgrims
worked very hard all
spring and summer.
That fall, the Pilgrims had a good harvest.
Because of Squanto's help,
they would have plenty to eat
through the winter.
They would also have warm homes.

The Pilgrims wanted to celebrate.
They wanted to give thanks.
They decided to have a feast.
They sent Squanto to invite an
Indian chief named Massasoit
to their dinner.
They thought that Massasoit might
bring a few people with him.

Thanksgiving feasts were not
new to the Indians.
Their feast was called the
Green Corn Dance.
It was a huge feast.
So Massasoit brought 90 people
to the Pilgrims' Thanksgiving feast.
The Pilgrims were very surprised.
But they tried not to show it.
There were 55 Pilgrims and 92 Indians.
That made 147 people!
The Pilgrims were not sure they had
enough food for everyone.
They had to get busy!

For three days, the women
did nothing but cook.

When the day for the feast arrived, everything was ready.

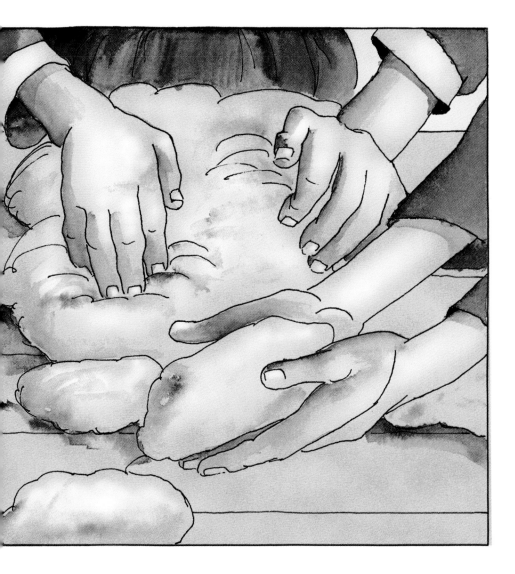

What a feast it was!

The Indians had brought five deer.

The women made these into stew.

They roasted turkeys,

geese, and ducks.

They cooked lobsters, eels, clams, oysters, and fish.

They made biscuits and bread.

They roasted corn for hoe cakes.

They boiled corn with molasses to
make Indian pudding.
There was plenty of dried fruit
for everyone.

Popcorn balls were invented by
the Indians in that area.
So there may even have been
popcorn balls.

Usually, the Pilgrims thought games
were a waste of time.
But on this day they played.
The men held contests.
They leaped and jumped and raced.

Everyone showed off.

The Pilgrims marched.

The Indians shot arrows.

And people ate until they

could hardly move.

What a happy day that first
Thanksgiving was.

The Pilgrims had new, warm homes.

They had new friends and plenty of food.

They knew they would be able to live
through the next winter.

And none of it would have happened
without a Patuxet Indian
named Squanto.

Afterword

Things did not turn out to be as easy as they looked on that first Thanksgiving. The winter that followed was even worse than the first for the Pilgrims. Then three more ships sailed into Plymouth. They brought hundreds of people, but no food. The crop in 1622 was not a good one, so there was no Thanksgiving that year. Thanksgiving was celebrated again in 1623, but it was celebrated in July to give thanks for rain.

For years, there was no official day for Thanksgiving. People celebrated it whenever they felt like it. Then in 1864, President Lincoln named the last Thursday in November as the official U.S. Thanksgiving. In 1939, President Roosevelt changed it to the third Thursday. Then, in 1941, it was changed back again.